Czech Medieval Mandolin

Ondřej Šárek

Contents

ISBN-13: 978-1501046711
ISBN-10: 1501046713

Introduction

The book contains 15 monophonic and 6 polyphonic compositions which were cretaed and played in the Czech area during the Medieval.

Vast majority of pieces is sacred but there ate four secular compositions, too (page no.4, 8, 17 and 21) and two instrumental music (page no. 9 and 16).

Wishinh you lovely time with Medieval music.

How to read tablature

Score

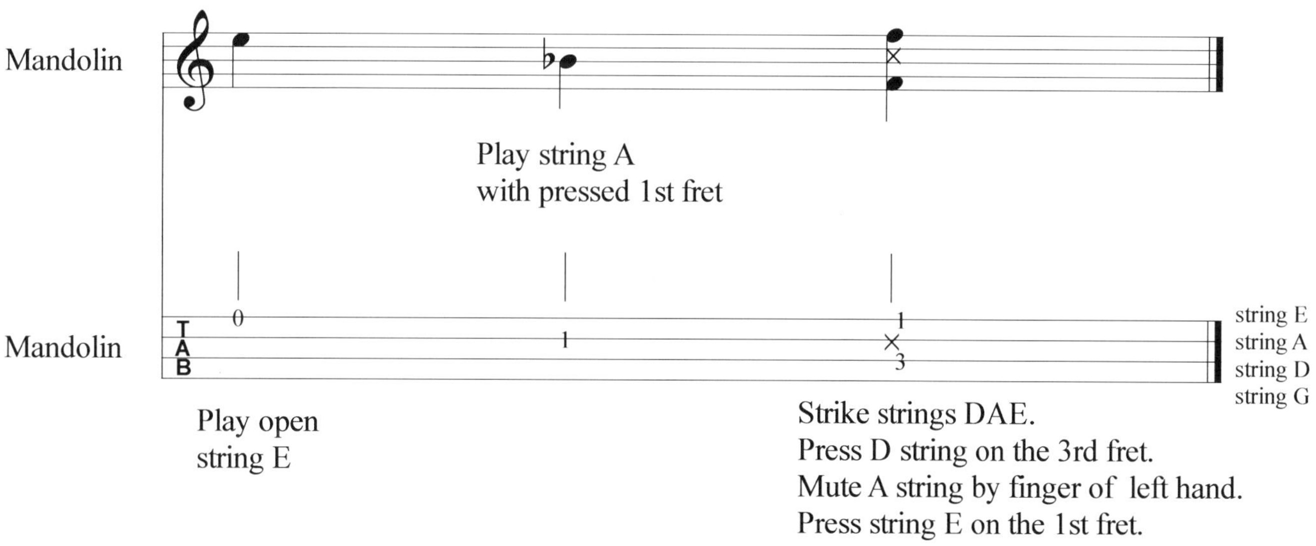

Andělíku rozkochaný

Score

Vyšehradský sborník cca 1396
arr: Ondřej Šárek

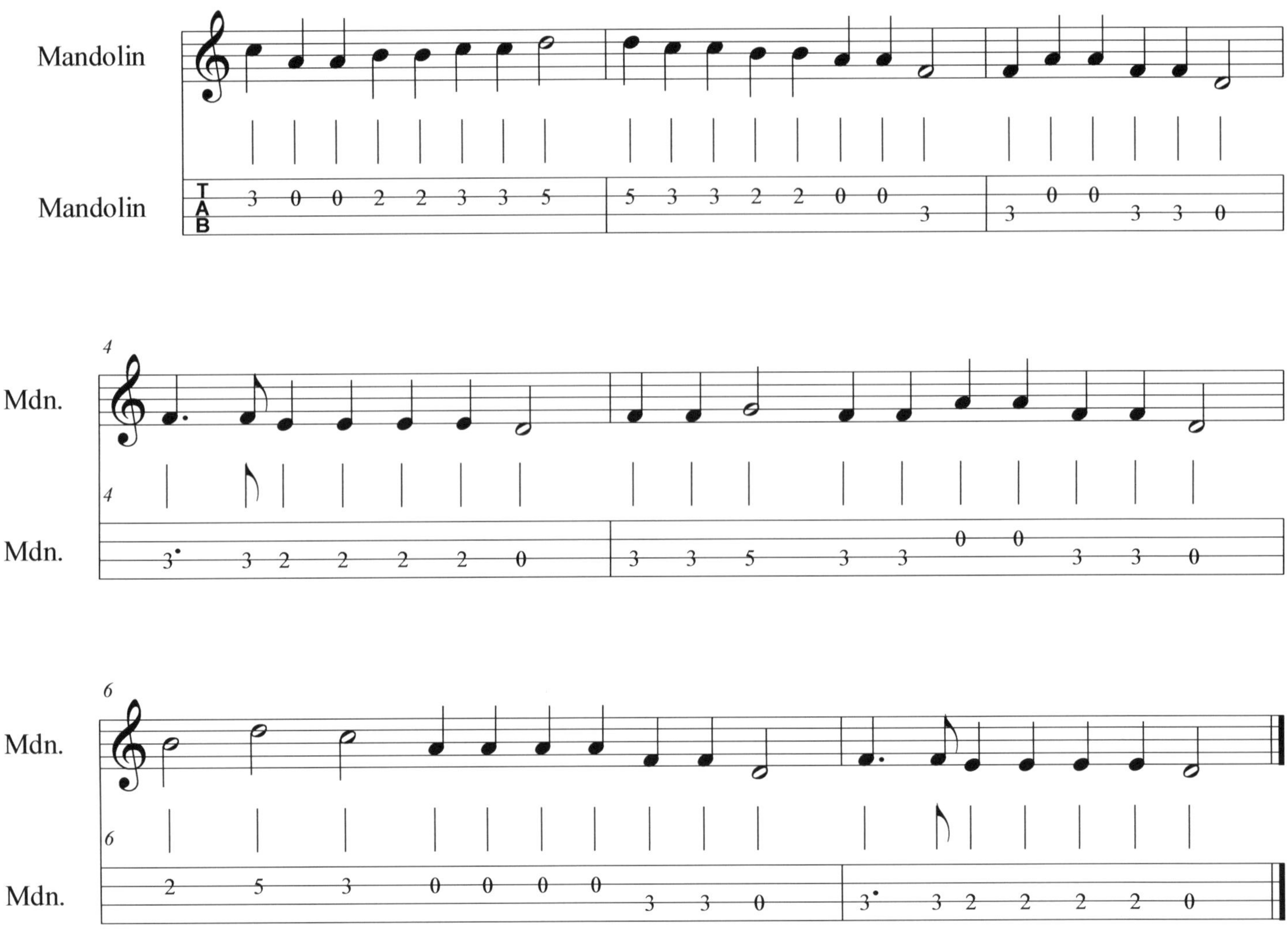

Ave maris stella

Score

Vyšebrodský rukopis cca 1410
arr: Ondřej Šárek

Buóh všemohúcí

Score

Jistebnický kancionál cca 1420
arr: Ondřej Šárek

Buóh všemohúcí

Score

manuscript beginning of the 14th century
arr: Ondřej Šárek

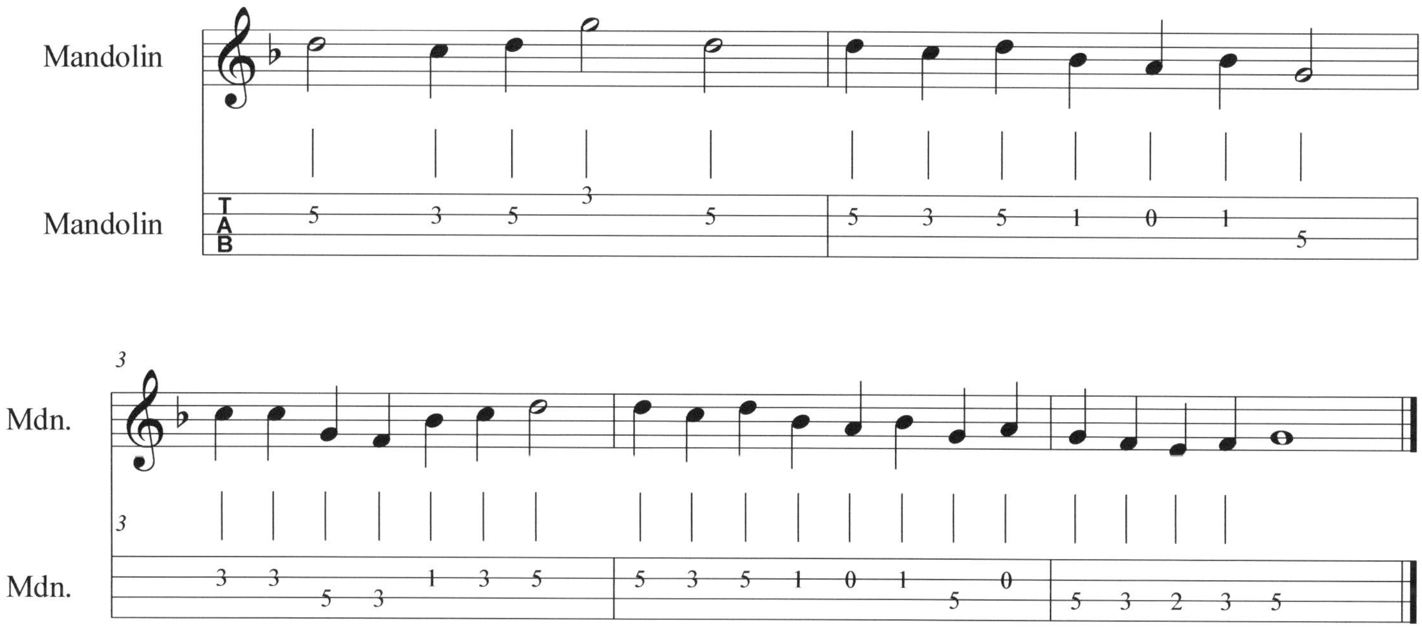

Jezu Kriste, štědrý kněže

Score

Jistebnický kancionál cca 1420
arr: Ondřej Šárek

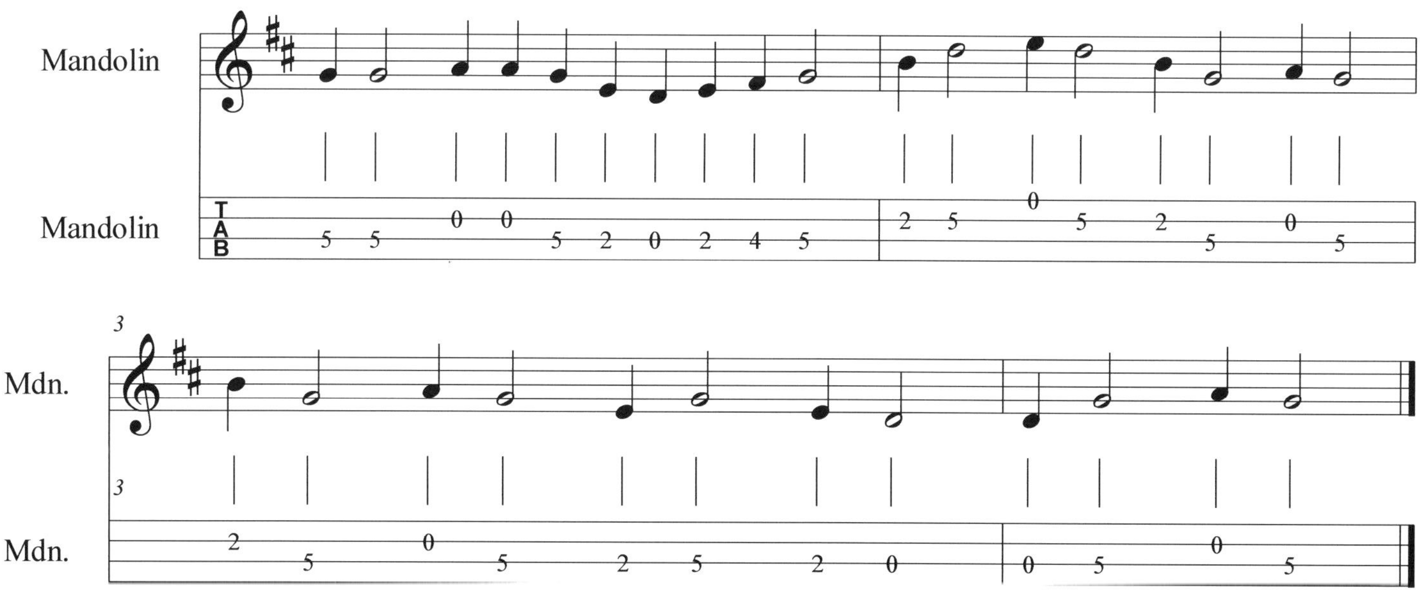

Dřevo sě listem odieva

Score

manuscript from the late 14th century
arr: Ondřej Šárek

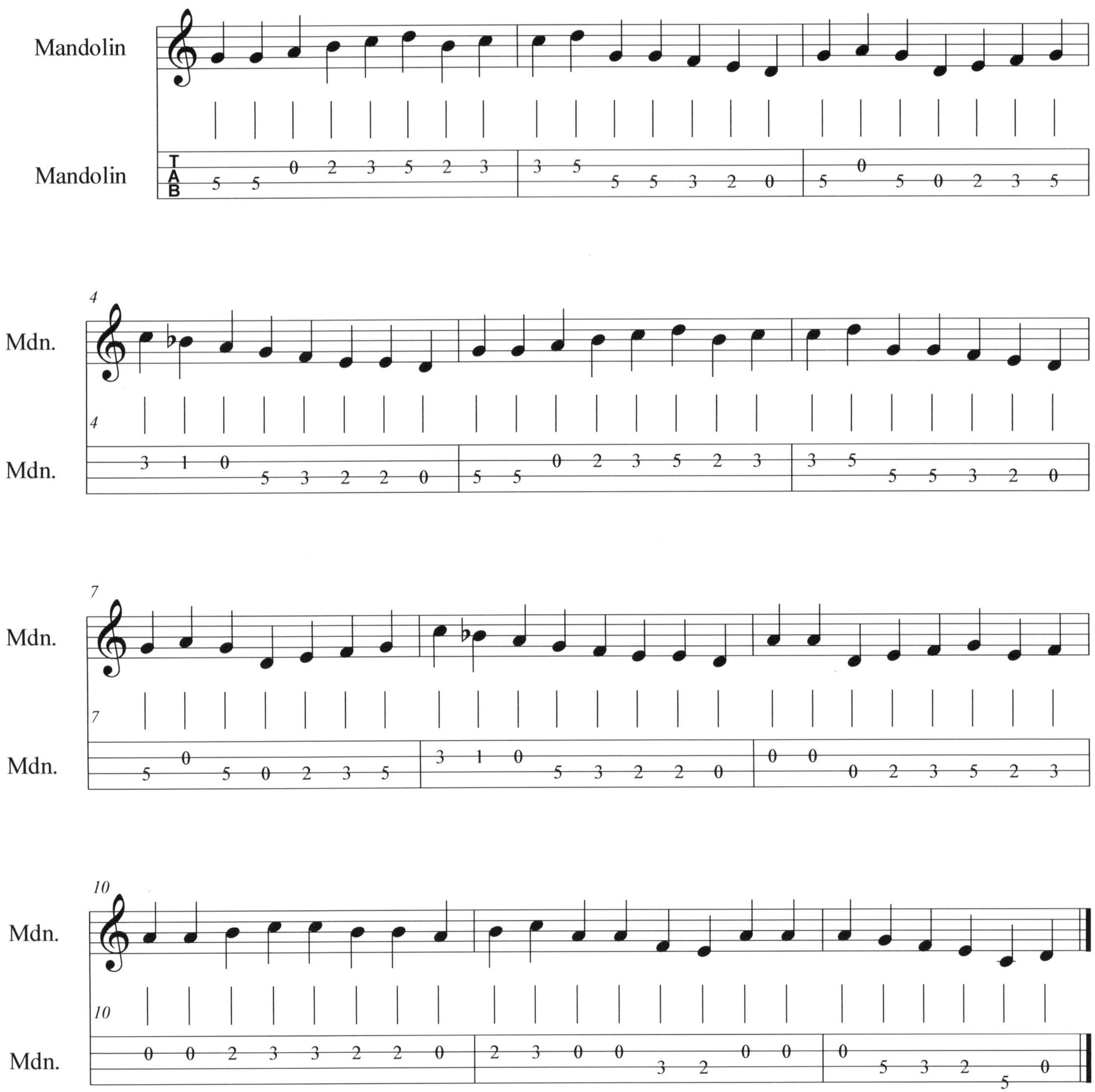

Czaldy waldy

Score

Vyšehradský sborník cca 1396
arr: Ondřej Šárek

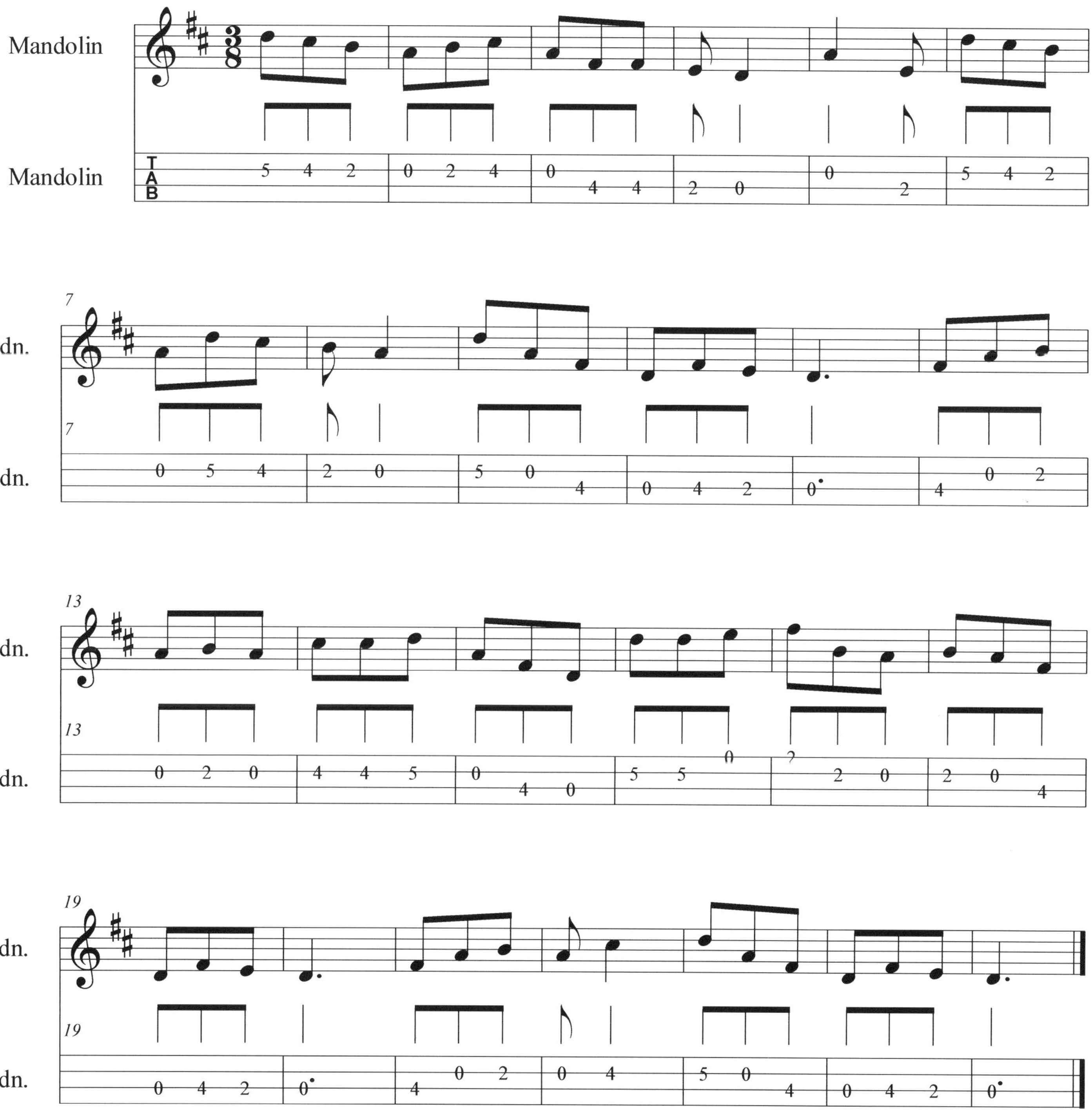

Ex legis observantia

Score

Vyšebrodský rukopis cca 1410
arr: Ondřej Šárek

Score

Hospodine, pomiluj ny

the turn of 10/11th century
arr: Ondřej Šárek

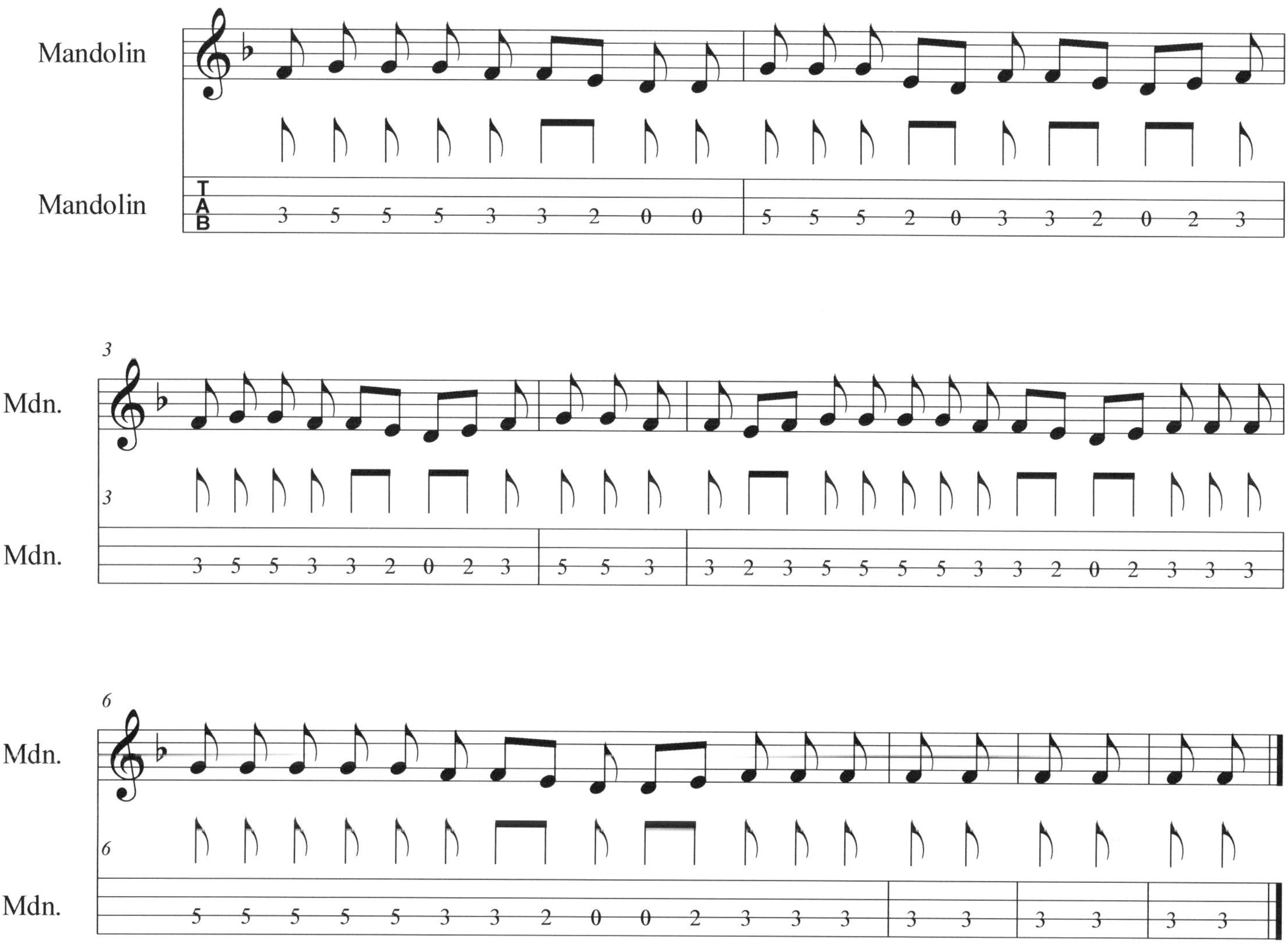

Divo flagrans

Score

Vyšebrodský rukopis cca 1410
arr: Ondřej Šárek

Mdn.

In hoc anni circulo

Score

Jistebnický kancionál cca 1420
arr: Ondřej Šárek

Ježíš, náš spasitel

Score

Jistebnický kancionál cca 1420
arr: Ondřej Šárek

Ktož jsú boží bojovníci

Score

Jistebnický kancionál cca 1420
arr: Ondřej Šárek

16
Mdn.
16
Mdn.
21
Mdn.
21
Mdn.
25
Mdn.
25
Mdn.
29
Mdn.
29
Mdn.

Score

Lidový tanec

Vyšehradský sborník cca 1396
arr: Ondřej Šárek

More festi querimus

Score

Jistebnický kancionál cca 1420
arr: Ondřej Šárek

Navščěv nás, Kriste žádúcí

Score

cca 1380
arr: Ondřej Šárek

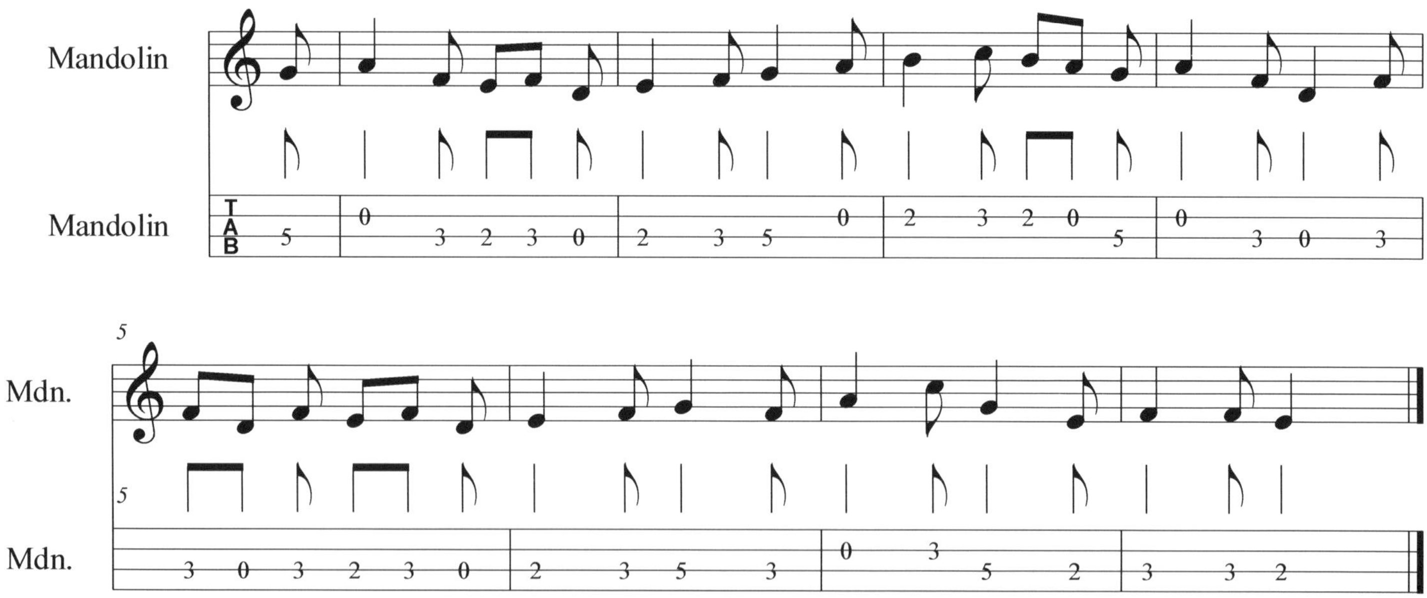

Rotulum Sanctus

Score

Vyšehradský rukopis cca 1450
arr: Ondřej Šárek

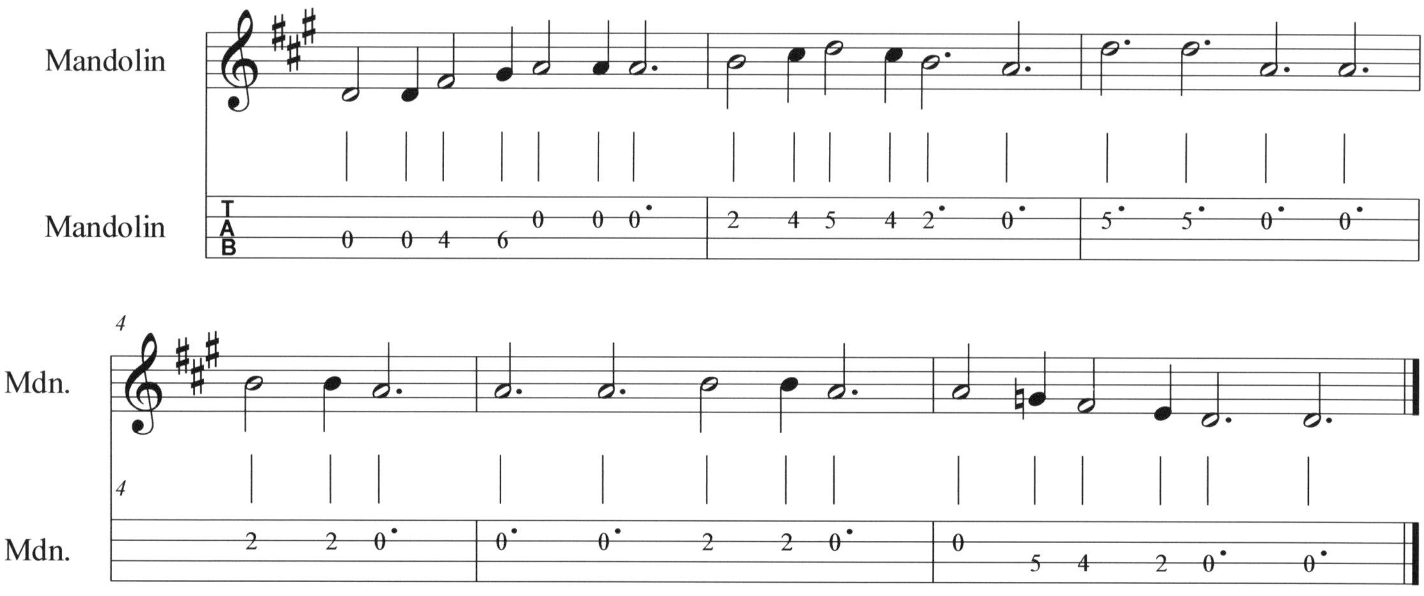

Povstaň, povstaň, Veliké Město pražské

Score

Jistebnický kancionál cca 1420
arr: Ondřej Šárek

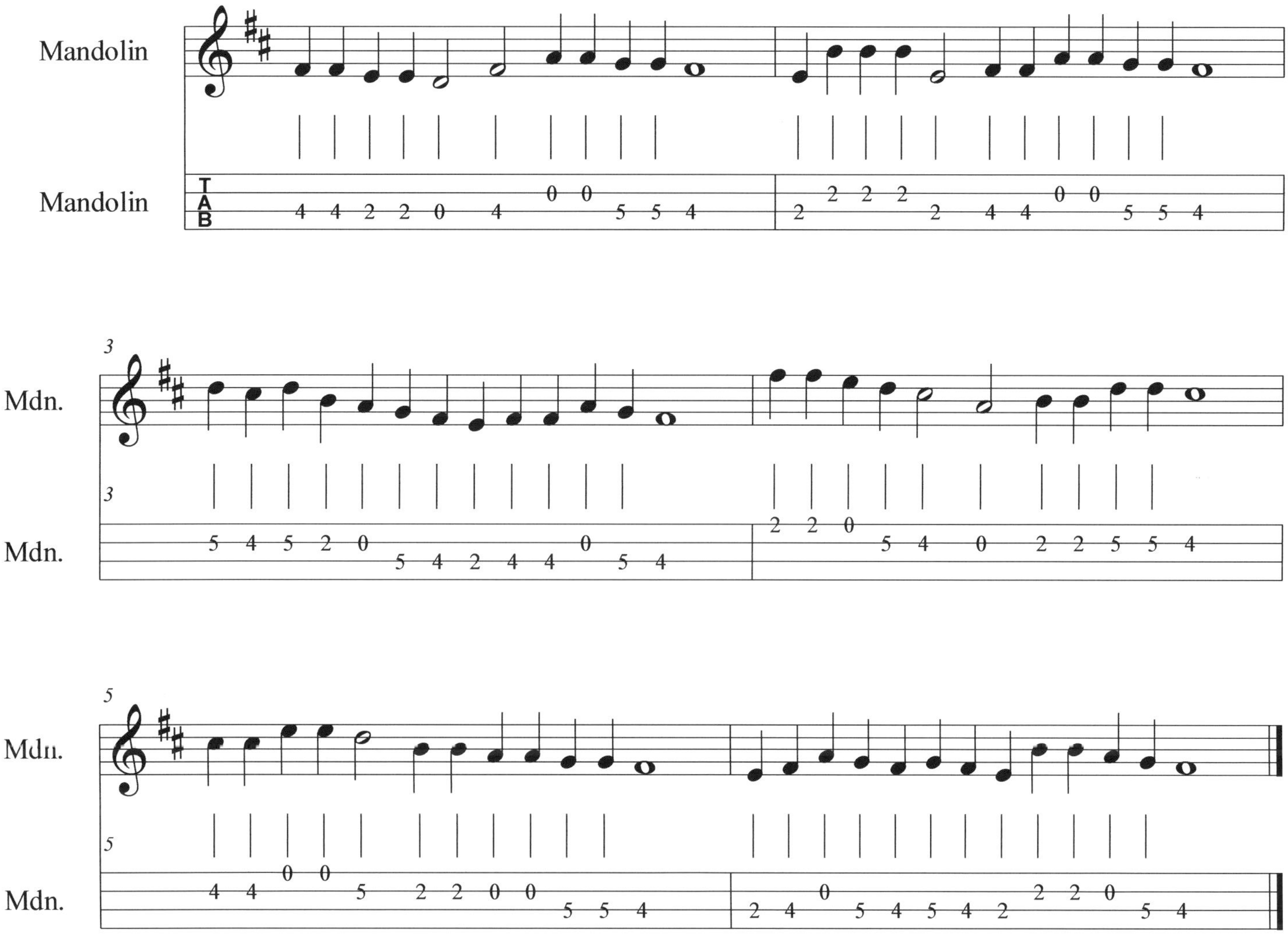

Tropus super Regina

Score

Vyšehradský rukopis cca 1450
arr: Ondřej Šárek

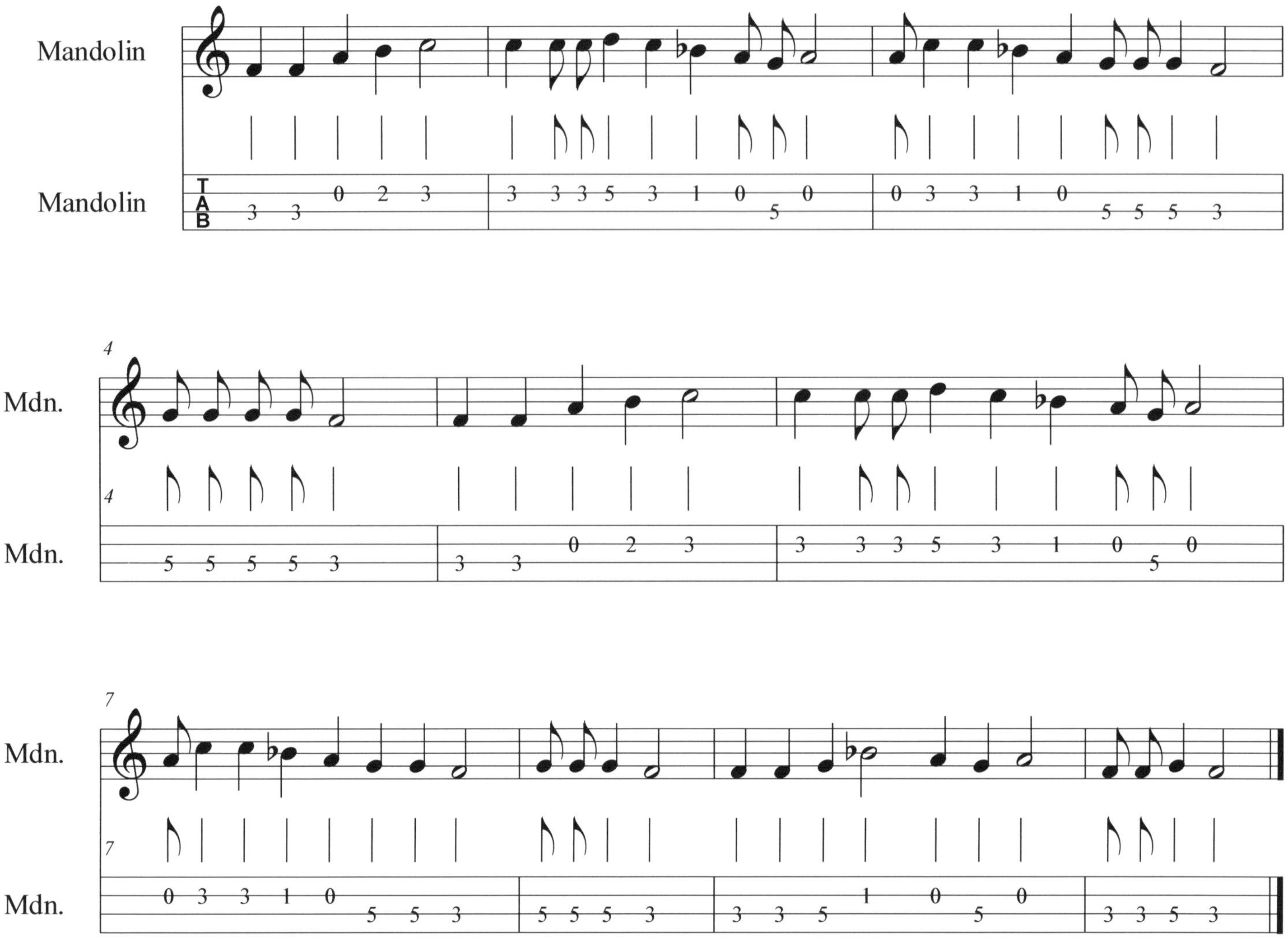

Svatý Václave

Score

cca 1280
arr: Ondřej Šárek

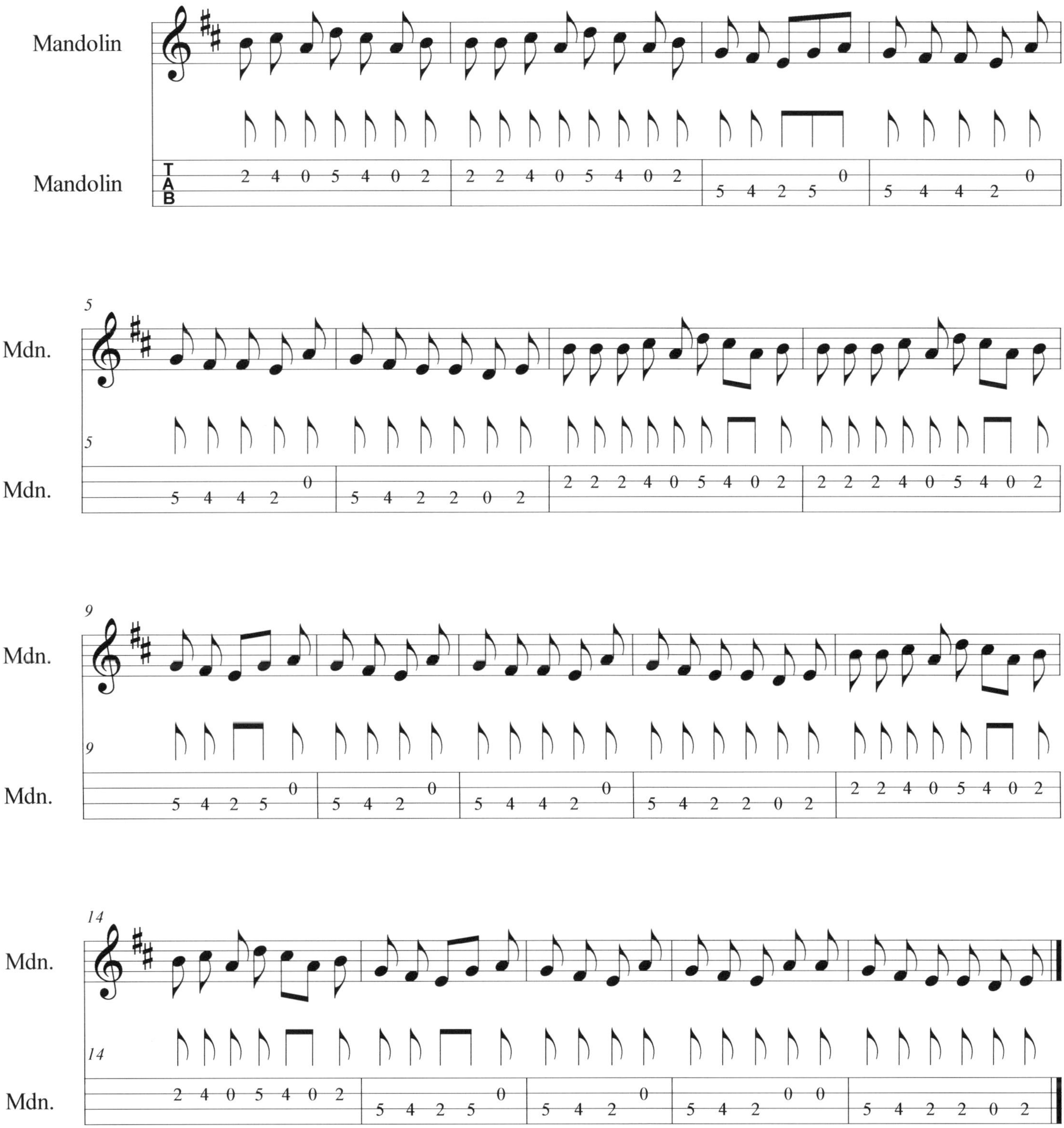

Guitalele (Guitarlele)

Fingerpicking Guitalele Solo volume I. (CSI)
Fingerpicking Guitalele Solo volume II. (CSI)
Fingerpicking Guitalele Solo volume III. (CSI)
Gregorian chant for Guitalele (CSI)
The Czech Lute for Guitalele (CSI)
Irish tunes for Guitalele (CSI)
The canons for Guitalele (CSI)
Fingerpicking Guitalele Solo volume IV. (CSI)
Fingerpicking Guitalele Solo volume V. - Classical music (CSI)
Czech Medieval Guitalele (CSI)

Cut Capo (Partial Capo) Guitar

Cut capo flatpicking guitar songbook Gospel and Hymns I. (CSI)
Cut capo flatpicking guitar songbook Gospel and Hymns II. (CSI)
Cut capo flatpicking guitar songbook Christmas Carols (CSI)
Cut capo flatpicking guitar songbook Jewish songs (CSI)
Cut capo flatpicking guitar songbook Gregorian chant (CSI)
Cut capo flatpicking guitar songbook Children's Songs (CSI)

DADGAD Guitar

Czech Medieval DADGAD Guitar (CSI)
The canons for DADGAD Guitar (CSI)
Fingerpicking DADGAD Guitar Solo (CSI)
The Czech Lute for DADGAD Guitar (CSI)
Gregorian chant for DADGAD Guitar (CSI)
Gregorian chant for flatpicking EADGBE Guitar (CSI)

EADEAE Guitar

Fingerpicking EADEAE Guitar Solo (CSI)

New Anglo Concertina books

For C/G 30-button Wheatstone Lachenal System

Gospel Anglo Concertina Solos (CSI)
Notebook for Anna Magdalena Bach and Anglo Concertina (CSI)
Robert Burns songs for Anglo Concertina (CSI)
The Czech Lute for Anglo Concertina (CSI)
Gregorian chant for Anglo Concertina (CSI)

For C/G 20-button

Gospel C/G Anglo Concertina Solos (CSI)
Robert Burns songs for C/G Anglo Concertina (CSI)
Gregorian chant for Anglo Concertina (CSI)

Mandolin

Czech Medieval Mandolin (CSI)
Gregorian chant for flatpicking Mandolin (CSI)

EADGBE Guitar

Czech Medieval EADGBE Guitar (CSI)
Gregorian chant for flatpicking EADGBE Guitar (CSI)

New Diatonic Accordion (Melodeon) books

For G/C diatonic accordion

Bass songbook for G/C melodeon (CSI)
Cross row style songbook for beginner
G/C diatonic accordion (CSI)
Gospel G/C diatonic accordion Solos (CSI)

For C/F diatonic accordion

Cross row style songbook for beginner
C/F diatonic accordion (CSI)
Gospel C/F diatonic accordion Solos (CSI)

For D/G diatonic accordion

Cross row style songbook for beginner
D/G diatonic accordion (CSI)
Gospel D/G diatonic accordion Solos (CSI)

New Ukulele books

For C tuning ukulele

Classics for Ukulele (MB)
Ukulele Bluegrass Solos (MB)
Antonin Dvorak: Biblical Songs (CSI)
Irish tunes for all ukulele (CSI)
Gospel Ukulele Solos (CSI)
Gregorian chant for Ukulele (CSI)
The Czech Lute for Ukulele (CSI)
Romantic Pieces by Frantisek Max Knize for Ukulele (CSI)
Notebook for Anna Magdalena Bach and Ukulele (CSI)
Open Tunings for Ukulel (MB)
Robert Burns songs for ukulele (CSI)
Jewish songs for C tuning ukulele (CSI)
Campanella style songbook for beginner: C tuning ukulele (CSI)
Antonín Dvořák: opera The Jacobin for ukulele ((CSI)
Leopold Mozart's Notebook for Wolfgang Arranged for Ukulele (MB)
The canons for one or two ukuleles (CSI)
Solo and Variations for ukulele *volume 1., 2., 3.* (CSI)
Czech Medieval Ukulele (CSI)

For C tuning with low G

Irish tunes for all ukulele (CSI)
Gospel Ukulele low G Solos(CSI)
Antonin Dvorak: Biblical Songs: for Ukulele with low G (CSI)
Gregorian chant for Ukulele with low G (CSI)
The Czech Lute for Ukulele with low G (CSI)
Romantic Pieces by Frantisek Max Knize for Ukulele with low G (CSI)
Notebook for Anna Magdalena Bach and Ukulele with low G (CSI)
Robert Burns songs for ukulele with low G (CSI)
Jewish songs for ukulele with low G (CSI)
Campanella style songbook for beginner: ukulele with low G (CSI)
Czech Medieval Ukulele with low G (CSI)

For Baritone ukulele

Irish tunes for all ukulele (CSI)
Gospel Baritone Ukulele Solos (CSI)
Antonin Dvorak: Biblical Songs: for Baritone Ukulele (CSI)
Gregorian chant for Baritone Ukulele (CSI)
The Czech Lute for Baritone Ukulele (CSI)
Romantic Pieces by Frantisek Max Knize for Baritone Ukulele (CSI)
Notebook for Anna Magdalena Bach and Baritone Ukulele (CSI)
Robert Burns songs for Baritone ukulele (CSI)
Jewish songs for baritone ukulele (CSI)
Campanella style songbook for beginner: Baritone ukulele (CSI)
Czech Medieval Baritone Ukulele (CSI)

For Baritone ukulele with high D

Jewish songs for baritone ukulele with high D (CSI)
Campanella style songbook for beginner: Baritone ukulele with high D (CSI)
Solo and Variations for Baritone ukulele with high D *volume 1., 2., 3.* (CSI)

For 6 sting ukulele (Lili'u ukulele)

Gospel 6 string Ukulele Solos (CSI)
Gregorian chant for 6 string Ukulele (CSI)
Notebook for Anna Magdalena Bach and 6 string Ukulele (CSI)
Robert Burns songs for 6 string ukulele (CSI)

For Slide ukulele (lap steel ukulele)

Comprehensive Slide Ukulele: Guidance for Slide Ukulele Playing (CSI)
Gospel Slide Ukulele Solos (CSI)
Irish tunes for slide ukulele (CSI)
Robert Burns songs for Slide ukulele (CSI)

For D tuning ukulele

Skola hry na ukulele (G+W s.r.o.)
Irish tunes for all ukulele (CSI)
Jewish songs for D tuning ukulele (CSI)
Campanella style songbook for beginner: D tuning ukulele (CSI)

Ukulele Duets

Notebook for Anna Magdalena Bach, C tuning ukulele and C tuning ukulele (CSI)
Notebook for Anna Magdalena Bach, C tuning ukulele and Ukulele with low G (CSI)
Notebook for Anna Magdalena Bach, C tuning ukulele and Baritone ukulele (CSI)
Notebook for Anna Magdalena Bach, Ukulele with low G and Ukulele with low G (CSI)
Notebook for Anna Magdalena Bach, Ukulele with low G and Baritone ukulele (CSI)
Notebook for Anna Magdalena Bach, Baritone ukulele and Baritone ukulele (CSI)
The canons for one or two ukuleles (CSI)

Publishing House
CSI = CreateSpace Independent Publishing Platform
MB = Mel Bay Publications
G+W = G+W s.r.o.

Printed in Great Britain
by Amazon

54854994R00016